Crafts

Beading

Bracelets, Barrettes, and Beyond

by Thiranut Boonyadhistarn

Capstone press®

Mankato, Minnesota

Snap Books are published by Capstone Press,
151 Good Counsel Drive, P.O. Box 669, Mankato, Minnesota 56002.
www.capstonepress.com

Library of Congress Cataloging-in-Publication Data
Boonyadhistarn, Thiranut.
    Beading : bracelets, barrettes, and beyond / by Thiranut
Boonyadhistarn.
      p. cm.—(Snap books. Crafts)
    Summary: "A do-it-yourself crafts book for children and
pre-teens on beading"—Provided by publisher.
    Includes bibliographical references and index.
    ISBN-13: 978-0-7368-6472-5 (hardcover)
    ISBN-10: 0-7368-6472-5 (hardcover)
    1. Beadwork—Juvenile literature. I. Title. II. Series.
TT860.B653 2007
745.58'2—dc22   2006004102

Editor: Megan Schoeneberger
Designer: Bobbi J. Wyss
Production Artist: Renée T. Doyle
Photo Researcher: Kelly Garvin

Photo Credits:
Aubrey Whitten, 32; Capstone Press/Karon Dubke, cover (objects), 10 (colored pins), 14 (jewelry), 19, 21 (jewelry);
Capstone Press/TJ Thoraldson Digital Photography, cover (girl), 4 (all), 5 (all), 6 (all), 8–9, 10 (silver pins and bracelet),
11 (all), 12 (all), 13 (all), 14 (tools and supplies), 15, 16 (all), 17, 18 (all), 21 (hands), 22, 23, 24, 25, 27 (all); Corbis/epa/Mike
Nelson, 29 (left); Getty Images Inc./Hulton Archive/MPI, 28 (right); Shutterstock/Garth Helms, 28 (left)

Capstone Press wishes to thank Sonja Swenson, owner of Sticks & Stones beading shop in Mankato, Minnesota,
for her help in preparing this book.

1 2 3 4 5 6 11 10 09 08 07 06

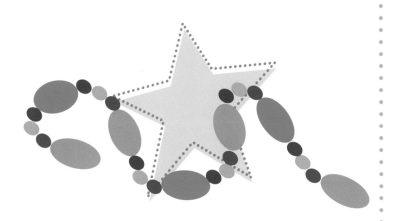

Table of Contents

CHAPTER 1 Show Off Your Style.............4

CHAPTER 2 Pliers and Wires 6

CHAPTER 3 Pin It Down........................8

CHAPTER 4 Get Wired 12

CHAPTER 5 Beads to the Rescue...............16

CHAPTER 6 Bead It and Bag It 18

CHAPTER 7 Wild and Wacky Beads.............22

CHAPTER 8 Charmed, I'm Sure.................24

Fast Facts 28

Glossary 30

Read More.....................................31

Internet Sites 31

About the Author 32

Index 32

Go Metric!

It's easy to change measurements to metric! Just use this chart.

To change	into	multiply by
inches	centimeters	2.54
inches	millimeters	25.4
feet	meters	.305
yards	meters	.914
ounces (liquid)	milliliters	29.57
ounces (liquid)	liters	.029
cups (liquid)	liters	.237
pints	liters	.473
quarts	liters	.946
gallons	liters	3.78
ounces (dry)	grams	28.35
pounds	grams	453.59

CHAPTER 1

Show Off Your Style

So many beads, never enough time.

Want to add a little flash to your wardrobe? You could buy necklaces, bracelets, and other **accessories** in stores. They're okay, but they're not exactly unique, are they? If you really want your personal style to sparkle, try making your own accessories with beads.

Just head to a beading or craft store. You'll find all kinds of beads, from tiny, shiny **seed beads** to funky, chunky clay beads. Plastic beads. Wooden beads. Fake pearl or fake crystal. Any color you can imagine. The world of beading is full of choices. You'll never look ordinary again.

Don't Mix Your Beads

It's a real pain when your beads get all mixed up. So how do you keep them separate? You could go to the store and buy a plastic craft tray with compartments for keeping small items separate. But another great idea is to put your beads in empty baby food jars or spice jars.

CHAPTER 2

Pliers and Wires

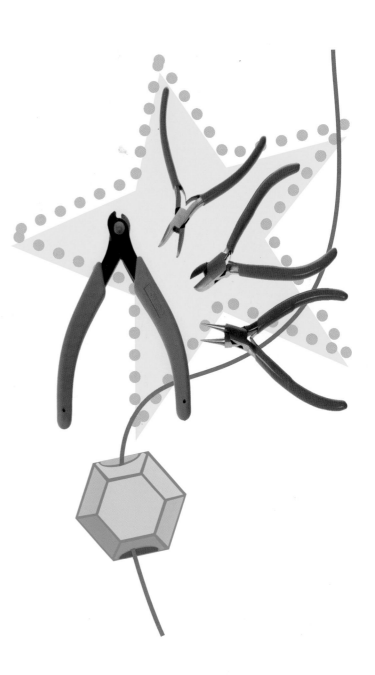

You need only a few simple tools and spools to get started.

Browse through any beading store, and you'll find what seems like a zillion kinds of strange-looking tools, strings, clasps, and other unrecognizable objects. But hold on to your wallet. You don't need to buy them all to enjoy beading. You can make all the projects in this book with just a handful of basic tools and **findings**.

Tools

bent-nose pliers—tool used to hold jewelry while you're working on it, or for opening and closing jump rings

memory wire cutter—tool made specifically for cutting extra-hard memory wire

round-nose pliers—tool used for looping and twisting wire and pins

wire cutter—tool for cutting standard beading wire and pins

Wires and Cords

beading wire—bendable wire in various **gauges**, usually available by the **spool**

elastic cord—plastic- or fabric-covered stretch cord used for beading

memory wire—very hard wire made to hold its spiral shape

Findings

eye pin—wire pin with a small, closed loop at one end

head pin—wire pin with a small, flat head at one end

jump ring—small ring used to attach links and clasps in pieces of jewelry

lobster claw and **spring ring**—clasps used for bracelets and necklaces

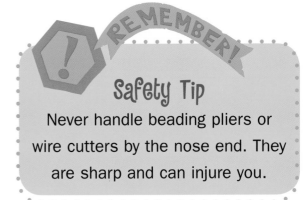

REMEMBER!

Safety Tip

Never handle beading pliers or wire cutters by the nose end. They are sharp and can injure you.

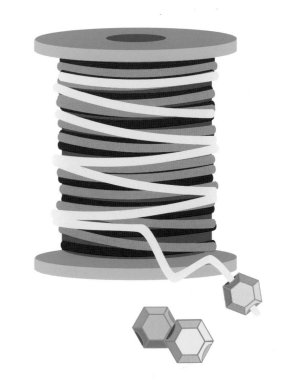

CHAPTER 3

Pin It Down

Who knew safety pins could be so cool?

Time to clean out your junk drawers. Then check out your laundry room or your mom's sewing kit. You're going to need safety pins—lots of them—for this fab and funky beaded bracelet. Nobody will ever believe that it started out as a pile of plain old safety pins.

Pins with Pizzazz

Dress up your bracelets even more by using colored safety pins. You'll find them in fabric stores, quilting shops, and even the sewing section in some department stores. Look for colors that range from pastels to jewel tones.

Here's what you need

* 60 to 80 1-inch or 2-inch safety pins (the number depends on the size of your wrist)
* seed beads
* mixed beads
* 2 sections of elastic beading cord, 24 inches long
* scissors

Here's what you do

1 Open half of the pins. Thread seed beads to fill the point, and refasten. Set them aside.

2 Thread the larger mixed beads onto the rest of the pins, and refasten.

3 Tie double knots about 6 inches from the end of each section of cord.

4 String one section of cord through the top of a seed bead pin. Then string the cord through the bottom of a mixed bead pin. Continue stringing the pins, alternating in this way, until all pins are on the cord.

5 String the other cord section through the other side of the safety pins.

6 Lift up the bracelet by the cord ends. The pins should hang in the middle, sort of like a hammock.

7 Tie the ends of the top section of cord together with a double knot. Repeat with the bottom section of string.

8 Cut off the extra cord, and your new bracelet is ready to wear.

Stretch Your String

The elastic cord you use in this project is really flexible for making lots of other jewelry. And you don't need any findings or clasps. To make simple necklaces, bracelets, or anklets, cut a piece of elastic cord at least 6 inches longer than what you'll need. Tie a double knot 3 inches from one end and thread beads onto the other end. Then tie the ends together with a double knot and cut off the extra cord.

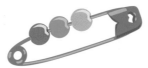

CHAPTER 4

Get Wired

Make your style unforgettable.

Regular wire cutter

Memory wire cutter

Who knew jewelry could have a memory? Memory wire actually remembers its shape. You don't even need any clasps or other findings. The jewelry just wraps into place. The wire comes in different widths to fit around your toe, ankle, finger, wrist, arm, and neck. Your wraparound jewelry will be totally fabulous.

Making the Cut

Ordinary wire cutters won't cut it for memory wire. Memory wire is too hard and will ruin regular wire cutters. Instead, use a cutter made just for memory wire.

Lead Me to the Beads

Having a tough time finding what you need to bead? You don't need to have a bead specialty store in your town. More and more craft stores are carrying large selections of beads and supplies. You can find tools like pliers, wire, and wire cutters at your local hardware store. And ask your parents if it's okay to log on. You'll find a lot of beads and supplies for sale on the Internet.

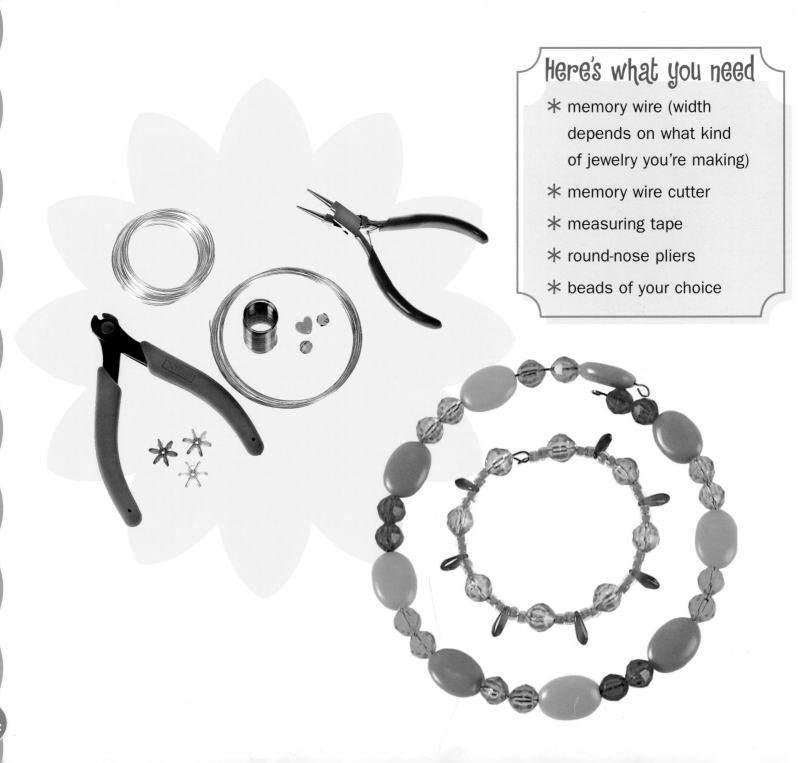

Here's what you need

* memory wire (width depends on what kind of jewelry you're making)
* memory wire cutter
* measuring tape
* round-nose pliers
* beads of your choice

Here's what you do

1 Using the memory wire cutter, cut a piece of wire for the jewelry you want to make. Remember that it should be long enough to wrap around the intended body part at least once. For armbands and anklets, the wire should be long enough to wrap around twice. No matter what kind of jewelry you're making, leave ¼ to ⅓ inch on each end for looping.

2 Using the round-nose pliers, make a small loop at one end of the wire.

3 Thread the beads onto the wire until you have about ½ inch of wire left. Trim the extra wire down to about ¼ to ⅓ inch.

4 Use the round-nose pliers to loop the end of the wire, and your piece is ready to wear.

Getting Loopy?

Looping wire and eye pins with round-nose pliers will take your jewelry designs in new directions. Remember that the size of the loop will depend on how far down on the nose of the pliers you are looping the wire. The closer to the handles, the larger the loop will be.

CHAPTER 5

Beads to the Rescue

Say goodbye to bad hair days.

Does your hair keep falling over your eyes? Maybe you're trying to grow your hair long, and it's looking a little shaggy. Or maybe you just want a new way to style your hair. You're going to love these one-of-a-kind barrettes. Beaded hair accessories are a hot item, and now you can make your own. This project will also work on hair combs or large hair clips.

Here's what you do

1 Cut a piece of wire about ½ inch longer than the barrette.

2 Loop one end of the wire by wrapping the tip of the wire around the round-nose pliers and twisting it.

3 Lay beads alongside the wire to see how many will fit. Then thread the ¼-inch beads onto the wire.

4 Loop the other end of the wire.

5 If the barrette is slightly curved, bend the beaded wire along the barrette to fit the curve. If the barrette is straight, make sure the wire is not bent.

6 Apply a generous amount of hot glue to the surface of the barrette, and carefully place the beaded piece on top of the glue. Allow 5 minutes for the glue to harden, and your barrette is ready to wear.

REMEMBER!
Safety Tip
Always remember to unplug hot glue guns immediately after you're done using them.

CHAPTER 6

Bead It and Bag It

Bag charms are all the rage.

Give your bag some extra flair. Hook a bag charm on your purse, book bag, or backpack. With your name on it, you'll never get your bag mixed up with someone else's. Everyone at school will know it's yours.

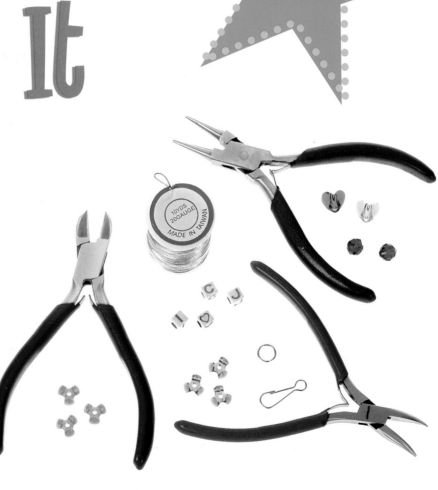

Here's what you need

* alphabet beads with the letters of your name

* variety of other beads of your choice

* 20-gauge beading wire

* ruler

* wire cutter

* round-nose pliers

* 1 jump ring, 10-millimeter size

* bent-nose pliers

* 1- or 1½-inch **lanyard hook**

Turn the page to get started.

Here's what you do

1 Arrange the alphabet beads to spell out your name.

2 Measure out a piece of wire long enough to fit all the letters plus a few additional beads. Add 1 inch for looping space, then cut the wire. The wire should be at least 4 inches long.

3 Make a small loop at one end of the wire as a closure.

4 Thread your beads onto the wire.

5 Use the wire cutter to cut the extra wire, leaving about ¼ to ⅓ inch at the top. Using the round-nose pliers, loop the top of the wire to close it.

6 Cut two more 4-inch sections of wire.

7 Make a small loop at the bottom of each piece.

8 Thread beads onto each piece of wire, cut off the excess wire, and loop the top.

9 Use the bent-nose pliers to attach the 10-millimeter jump ring to the top loop of each of the three beaded wires.

10 Attach the lanyard hook through the jump ring, and hook the charm to your favorite bag.

Get a Grip

Just how do you open and close those tiny jump rings? It's tricky, but with some practice, you'll get the hang of it. Just grip one side of the jump ring with bent-nose pliers. Hold the other side with your thumb and index finger. Now twist the sides to open the ring. To close the jump ring, twist it back the same way you opened it.

CHAPTER 7

Wild and Wacky Beads

Ovens aren't just for baking cookies anymore.

Bake a batch of colorful beads with **polymer clay**. This clay won't dry out while you work with it, but it hardens when you bake it. You'll find it in dozens of colors, so there's no end to the possibilities for your own custom jewelry.

Here's what you need

* cookie sheet
* aluminum foil
* polymer clay in your choice of colors
* ruler
* small knitting needle
* oven mitt

REMEMBER!

Safety Tip

Always follow the package instructions when baking polymer clay. Temperatures and times may vary from one brand to another. Polymer clay can give off dangerous fumes if it gets too hot.

Here's what you do

1 Cover cookie sheet with aluminum foil.

2 Shape the clay into balls, cubes, tubes, or any shape that will work as a bead. Experiment with mixing different colors and thicknesses of clay. A good size for clay beads is ¼- to ½-inch thick.

3 Gently push a small knitting needle through the center of each bead to make a hole. Twist the needle as you push, and pull it back out gently.

4 Smooth any rough clay near the holes.

5 Place each bead on the cookie sheet.

6 Preheat the oven according to the instructions on the clay packets.

7 When the oven is preheated, bake the beads for the specified time.

8 Allow the beads to cool for at least 30 minutes before using.

CHAPTER 8

Charmed, I'm Sure

Express yourself with a charm bracelet.

A beaded charm bracelet takes a little work, but it's worth it. Before you start, you'll want to find some charms that reflect who you are. Check out beading supply stores, craft stores, and sewing stores. They usually carry a good selection.

Junk to Funk

Old buttons. One half of a pair of earrings. A little bell that fell off your costume after the last dance recital. What do these things have in common? They all seem useless, at least at first. But remember, if it has a hole in it, you can add it to your charm bracelet. So little things like old jewelry and buttons make awesome charms. Keep your eyes open—you never know what you'll find!

Here's what you need

* section of large-link chain (long enough to fit comfortably around your wrist)
* 6 to 8 charms
* 12 to 20 head pins, 1-inch size
* sketching paper
* pencil
* variety of beads
* round-nose pliers
* bent-nose pliers
* 12 to 20 jump rings, 8-millimeter size
* 1 jump ring, 10-millimeter size
* lobster claw clasp or spring ring

Here's what you do

1 Lay the chain flat and space out the head pins and charms equally along its length, planning how many charms you want to use. Keep in mind when the head pins get beaded, they'll take up extra space.

2 Draw a quick sketch of the chain and where each beaded head pin and charm will be placed on the chain.

3 Thread beads onto each head pin, leaving ¼ to ⅓ inch of wire at the top.

4 Using the round-nose pliers, loop the top of each head pin to close it.

5 Following your sketch, use the bent-nose pliers to attach each head pin to the chain by threading an 8-millimeter jump ring through the loop of the head pin and then through a link on the chain.

6 Attach each charm to the chain the same way.

7 Attach the 10-millimeter jump ring to the last link on one end of the chain.

8 Thread an 8-millimeter jump ring through the small loop on the lobster claw clasp or spring ring, and attach it to the last link on the other end of the chain. Your charm bracelet is ready to wear.

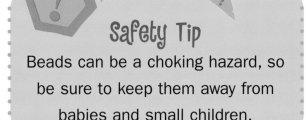

REMEMBER!
Safety Tip
Beads can be a choking hazard, so be sure to keep them away from babies and small children.

Fast Facts

The Eye of the Tiger

Tigereye is a brown and orange stone. When light reflects off its surface, it looks like a tiger's eye. Beads made from tigereye are thought to have a protective power. In ancient Rome, soldiers wore tigereye into battle for extra protection.

Valuable Beads

Before the first European settlers came to America, American Indians traded shell beads called wampum in ceremonies with other tribes. When the settlers arrived, they began trading for the beads. The beads became a form of money among the Indians and the settlers. Settlers even began making their own glass wampum beads, which were more valuable to the Indians.

A Portrait in Beads

Ancient Egyptians covered mummies with a net of beads woven to show what the person looked like in life. Most of these beads have been lost over thousands of years. But in March 2005, archaeologists found one mummy covered in colorful, shiny beads. The mummy is thought to be a man named Meri, a tutor of the king, who lived more than 4,000 years ago.

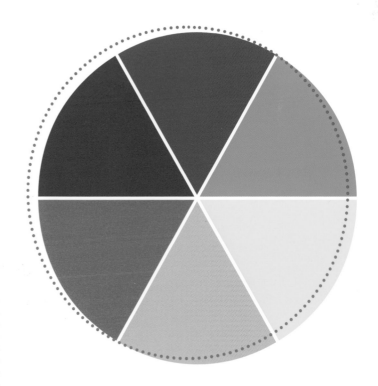

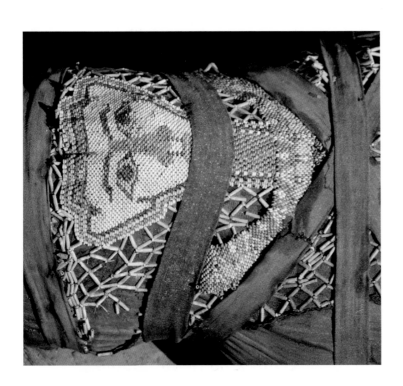

Color Wheel

Understanding color will help you make exciting and vibrant beading projects. This wheel shows how colors work with each other. The colors next to each other work together in harmony. Colors opposite each other have more contrast when used together.

29

Glossary

accessory (ak-SESS-uh-ree)—something, such as a belt or jewelry, that goes with your clothes

findings (FINDE-ingz)—small tools and supplies used by jewelers; findings include clasps, pins, ear hooks, and jump rings.

gauge (GAYJ)—the heaviness and width of beading wire

lanyard hook (LAN-yurd HUK)—a type of clasp used for attaching something to bags or straps

polymer clay (PAH-luh-muhr KLAY)—a type of plastic that can be sculpted like clay but does not dry out; polymer clay hardens when baked at certain temperatures.

seed bead (SEED BEED)—tiny bead made of glass

spool (SPOOL)—a wheel on which thread is wound

wampum (WAHM-puhm)—beads made from polished shells strung together or woven to make belts

Read More

Ashfield, Ben. *Beading for Fun!* For Fun! Minneapolis: Compass Point Books, 2005.

Bruder, Mikyla. *Bead Girl: Sparkly Projects from Tiaras to Toe Rings.* San Francisco: Chronicle Books, 2001.

Miller, Sharilyn. *Bead on a Wire: Making Handcrafted Wire and Beaded Jewelry.* Cincinnati: North Light Books, 2005.

Internet Sites

FactHound offers a safe, fun way to find Internet sites related to this book. All of the sites on FactHound have been researched by our staff.

Here's how:

1. Visit *www.facthound.com*
2. Choose your grade level.
3. Type in this book ID **0736864725** for age-appropriate sites. You may also browse subjects by clicking on letters, or by clicking on pictures and words.
4. Click on the **Fetch It** button.

FactHound will fetch the best sites for you!

About the Author

Thiranut Boonyadhistarn grew up in Tokyo, Bangkok, and Chicago. She learned various crafts in each country: origami in Japan, beading in Thailand, and paper crafts in America. The crafts she learned as a child have led to a lifelong love of the arts.

Boonyadhistarn has worked in film and TV production, graphic design, and book production. She also has written several kids' books on crafts. She lives in a tiny apartment in New York City, surrounded by boxes of glitter, rhinestones, and craft glue.

Index

bag charms, 18–21
barrettes, 16–17
beading wire, 7, 13, 15, 16, 17, 19, 20
beads, 4
    storage of, 5
    types of, 4, 22
    where to find, 13
bent-nose pliers, 7, 19, 20, 21, 26, 27

charm bracelet, 24, 26–27
color wheel, 29

elastic cord, 7, 10–11
eye pins, 7, 15

findings, 6, 7, 11, 12

head pins, 7, 26–27
hot glue gun, 16, 17

jump rings, 7, 19, 20, 21, 26, 27
    opening and closing, 21

lanyard hooks, 19, 20
lobster claws, 7, 26, 27
looping, 7, 15, 17, 20, 26

memory wire, 7, 12, 14–15
memory wire cutters, 7, 12, 14, 15

polymer clay, 22–23
polymer clay beads, 22–23

round-nose pliers, 7, 14, 15, 16, 17, 19, 20, 26

safety, 7, 17, 23, 27
safety pin bracelet, 8, 10–11
spring rings, 7, 26, 27

wampum, 28
wire cutters, 7, 12, 13, 16, 17, 19, 20